Printed in Great Britain
by Amazon

74695456R00068